Contents

Words in **bold** are in the glossary on pages 28–29.

Minibeasts at home

Some minibeasts make their homes in our homes. Others visit in search of food or shelter, or come in by accident.

House habitats

There can be several different types of **habitat** in a home. Under a sink it can be dark and damp. In the corner of a room it can be dry and warm. These habitats attract different minibeasts. Crumbs of food, carpets and our belongings can become their food.

This spider's body can grow up to 1 cm long.

▲ A house spider rests on a computer keyboard.

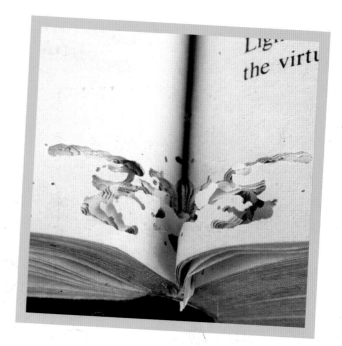

▶ Sometimes furniture beetle **larvae** become 'bookworms', eating holes through the pages.

What is a minibeast?

Minibeast is the name given to thousands of small **animals**. Although many are **insects**, others are not. Minibeasts do not have **backbones**, so scientists call them **invertebrates**. The ones that you are most likely to find in houses include spiders, wasps, flies, moths, ladybirds, woodlice, cockroaches and silverfish.

TOP TIP!

Look out for boxes like these because they will help you become a good minibeast spotter.

Friends or enemies?

Some minibeasts in our homes are **pests**, many are harmless and a few are useful. House spiders catch small flying insects, such as flies and mosquitoes, which we don't want inside. Hungry wasps and flies land on our food and may spread diseases. Other pests include beetles that eat the wood in our homes.

This housefly can grow up to 0.8 cm long.

◀ A housefly enjoys a plum. Flies like to eat our food.

Under the sink

Sometimes it is damp under the sink in the kitchen or bathroom. It is also dark and this kind of habitat attracts certain minibeasts.

Speedy silverfish

If you turn on the kitchen light in the evening, you might spot silverfish running for cover. These slim, silver insects have existed for 400 million years. In our homes they eat spilt flour, mould or even the glue that sticks wallpaper to the walls.

This silverfish can grow up to 1.8 cm long.

▲ Silverfish are wingless insects, with three long 'tails' at the end of the body.

▼ The hard shell of the woodlouse protects the soft body inside.

Harmless woodlice

Woodlice are harmless, **nocturnal** animals. They eat crumbs of food, flakes of dead skin and even their own droppings. Unlike the silverfish, they are **crustaceans** rather than insects and have 14 legs.

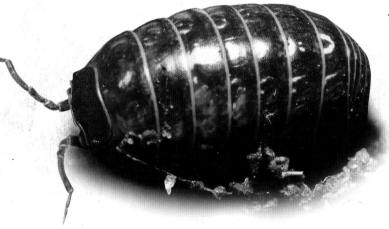

The pill woodlouse can grow up to 1.5 cm long.

This American cockroach can grow up to 4.5 cm long.

Cockroach pests

During the day, cockroaches rest around pipes, under floorboards or under the sink. Then at night they come out in search of food. They eat anything – meat, cheese, flour, pasta, bread. Cockroaches will even eat each other if there is nothing else around.

▲ Cockroaches carry dirt and disease on their feet and then spread them onto our food.

There are more than 4,000 types of cockroach worldwide and only 30 of them are pests. Cockroaches have been around since before the dinosaurs and were tough enough to survive the events that killed the dinosaurs.

Through the kitchen window

Leave the kitchen window open in the summer and flies are sure to buzz in. They can smell food and are looking for a good meal.

◀ A housefly flies towards a slice of bread.

A housefly can develop from egg to adult in 7 to 10 days. The female lays eggs in rubbish, uncovered food or a compost heap. The larvae hatch out and feed on whatever is close by. After a few days they turn into **pupae**, and then into adult flies.

▲ The fly larvae are white, the pupae are red-brown.

Food of all sorts

Houseflies have mouths that are like sponges, soaking up liquid food. The problem for us is that they are not fussy and they also eat rotting food or even animal droppings. When they move on to our food, their feet leave small bits of dirt and **bacteria** on what we are about to eat.

▶ These houseflies are feeding on uncovered ham. It is important to keep food covered to stop this from happening.

TOP TIP!

If you see flies buzzing around a compost heap or rubbish bin, there may be fly larvae inside. Don't touch – just look at them.

Hanging from the ceiling

Spiders are **arachnids**. They can surprise us by dropping down from the ceiling or running across the floor. Spiders eat flies, mosquitoes and other insects that we do not want in our homes.

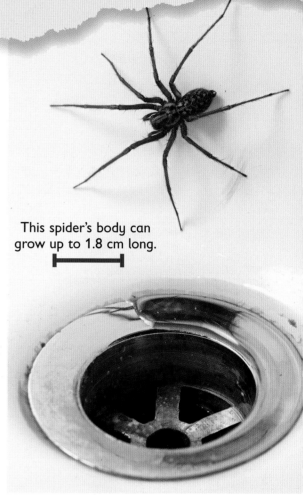

This spider's body can grow up to 1.8 cm long.

▶ House spiders often fall into the bath by accident and then cannot escape.

Spinning a web

A house spider has special body parts that make silk. The spider uses them to weave a web. Here it waits for an insect to walk or fly into the web. The insect sticks to the web and the spider injects it with poison.

◀ The spider feeds by sucking all the blood and juices out of its victim.

Spiderlings

When a female spider has met a male to mate with, the female lays eggs in a sac and attaches it to her web. When the eggs hatch, tiny spiderlings come out. After a few days, they spin fine silk lines that carry them away to new homes. The male stays with the female for a few more weeks and then dies. The female may then eat him!

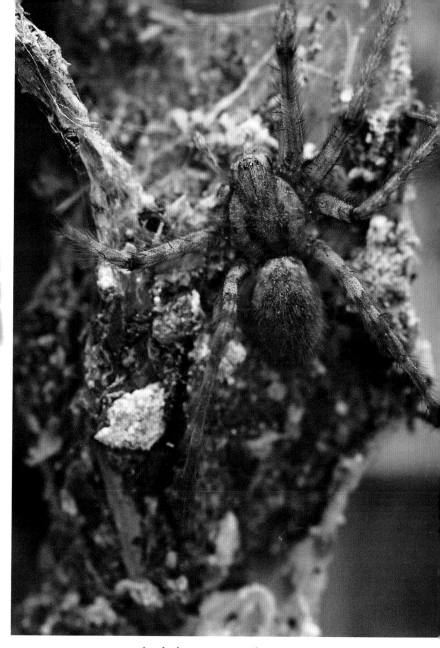

▲ A house spider protects its sac of spiderlings.

The harvestman is also an arachnid. It rests under windowsills or on walls during the day and then goes off hunting at night. It eats insect larvae and other small insects, dead or alive.

13

And now to bed

Some minibeasts are very unwelcome in our homes, especially the ones that like to live in our beds.

This bed bug can grow up to 0.5 cm long.

Biting bugs

Like all **bugs**, bed bugs are insects with special mouths for sucking. During the day, bed bugs hide away in bedding or behind the wallpaper. At night, they crawl onto the sleeping person, bite through his or her skin and suck up some blood. The bites are irritating but not dangerous.

▲ These oval brown insects move into bedrooms by travelling inside suitcases, clothing or bedding.

Another unwelcome minibeast in our bedrooms is the clothes moth. You are likely to see this small, brown moth in the summer months. The adult is harmless but it lays eggs on carpets, clothes or curtains. When the eggs hatch, the larvae (caterpillars) eat the fabric they are on, making holes.

This clothes moth larva can grow up to 0.5 cm long.

Dust mites

Most dust mites are too tiny to see without using a magnifying glass or **microscope**. These arachnids feed on flakes of dead skin that drop off our bodies all the time. Dust mites leave droppings behind them and it is the droppings that make some people itch or wheeze.

▼ This photograph of a dust mite has been magnified – made much bigger than real life.

This dust mite can grow up to 0.2 mm long.

Up in the roof

Up in the roof space of a house, you may find an amazing wasps' nest or signs of boring beetles.

The nest begins

Many types of wasp live alone, but others live in huge colonies, or nests. The **queen** starts the nest by choosing a good site, such as a roof space. She builds a small nest, lays some eggs and feeds the larvae when they hatch. The larvae turn into worker wasps which build the nest bigger and bigger. They also fetch food for the larvae that hatch from the queen's eggs.

This wasp can grow up to 1.8 cm long.

▼ Left undisturbed, wasps may build a huge nest in a roof space.

The nest

The wasps build their nest from paper. They scrape off bits of wood from fences, garden furniture or trees. They chew the wood and mix it with spit to make a paper **pulp**. The workers use the pulp to build hexagonal (six-sided) cells. Layers of paper pulp protect the cells on the outside.

▲ Each hexagonal cell contains one hungry larva that will turn into an adult wasp.

TOP TIP!

Many boring beetles and their **grubs** live in dead or dying trees. Look under the bark of fallen trees to see if you can see them, or the holes they have left behind.

Boring beetles

The death-watch beetle lays its eggs in the wood beams that hold up our homes. When the larvae hatch, they tunnel through the wood, eating it as they go. They can cause a lot of damage and can even make the building unsafe.

This death-watch beetle can grow up to 0.9 cm long.

◀ An adult death-watch beetle comes out of a hole it has made in some wood.

17

Under your feet

You will rarely see the tiny minibeasts that live in carpets and floorboards, but you may feel them sometimes.

Woodworm

Woodworm are not worms at all but the larvae, or grubs, of the furniture beetle. These small, brown beetles lay their eggs in wood. When they hatch, the larvae start eating out tiny tunnels through the wood – often our floorboards or furniture.

▲ A woodworm tunnels through a floorboard.

This woodworm can grow up to 0.6 cm long.
⊢⊣

This furniture beetle can grow up to 0.3 cm long.
⊢⊣

▶ People rarely see the adult furniture beetle.

Hopping fleas

The carpet on top of floorboards can get unwelcome visitors. These include insects called fleas. Fleas live on or close to pet dogs and cats. Sometimes they live in the carpet and hop onto whichever animal passes by – the cat, the dog or even you! They bite into the skin and suck out blood. As fast as they arrive, they hop off again.

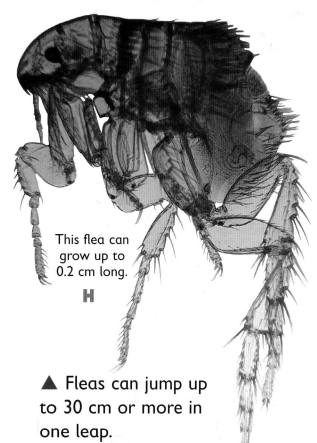

This flea can grow up to 0.2 cm long.

H

▲ Fleas can jump up to 30 cm or more in one leap.

Woolly bears

The larvae of the carpet beetle are also called woolly bears. While the adult beetle feeds on plant **pollen**, the larvae like to eat wool carpets and other fabrics.

This carpet beetle larva can grow up to 0.4 cm long.

H

▲ A woolly bear eating a rug.

In the summer, look out for ants running around the floor. They are usually just visiting in search of fallen crumbs of food. They carry the food back to their nest to feed hungry ant larvae.

Looking at minibeasts

Take a closer look at some of the minibeasts in your home or school by following these instructions.

You will need:
- Small plastic containers • A small paintbrush
- A magnifying glass • Paper and a pencil

What to do:
- Gently sweep any minibeasts in your home into plastic containers, using your paintbrush.

- Take a good look at each minibeast. How many legs does it have? Does it have wings? What colour is it? Use the magnifying glass to take a closer look. The identification guide on pages 26–27 may help you to name the minibeast.

- You could draw the minibeast or note down its size, number of legs, wings or **antennae.**

- Remember to return the minibeast to its home.

▼ Watch how a minibeast moves. Spiders can move very quickly on their long legs.

Wandering woodlice

Woodlice prefer to live in damp places. Try out this activity to test this fact.

You will need:
- A shoebox with a lid, or similar container • Some kitchen paper
- Water • A pencil • Woodlice

What to do:
- Take the shoebox and place a layer of damp kitchen paper in one corner.

- Make small holes in the lid with the pencil.

- Find some woodlice. Good places to search for them are under stones or logs, in compost heaps, under garden pots or in your house, if they live there.

- Gently place the woodlice in the shoebox, replace the lid and leave them for a few hours.

- Lift up the lid and see where the woodlice are resting.

Summer visitors

There are far more minibeasts around in the summer than the winter (see page 25). Some of them find their way into our homes by accident.

Moths and light

Moths fly through open doors and windows by accident on summer evenings. Confused, they often fly around as they try to find their way out again. If you open the window wide and turn off the light, they may fly outside again.

▲ A moth flutters around a light bulb.

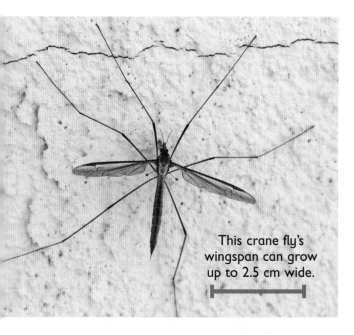

This crane fly's wingspan can grow up to 2.5 cm wide.

Daddy-long-legs

Daddy-long-legs are really called crane flies. They are harmless flies that find their way into our homes by accident. All crane flies live for only a week or two, mate, lay eggs in the ground and then die.

◀ Crane flies have long, thin legs that can fall off if touched.

Delicate lacewings

The pale-green lacewing is an insect with long antennae. It comes into homes, attracted by the light. It is completely harmless and is useful in the garden because it eats up plant-wrecking **aphids**.

This lacewing can grow up to 2 cm long.

◀ You can see the veins in the lacewing's wings.

Munching mosquitoes

Mosquitoes are unwelcome visitors to our homes. They fly into our bedrooms in search of a meal of human blood. Their sharp mouthparts pierce the skin so that they can suck up blood.

▼ Only the female mosquito feeds on blood.

This mosquito can grow up to 0.6 cm long.

Winter visitors

Many minibeasts lay eggs and then die at the end of the summer. Others **hibernate** underground, inside plant stems or find their way into our homes.

These ladybirds can grow up to 0.5 cm long.

Lines of ladybirds

Ladybirds can live for a year or two. They hibernate over the winter to survive. As the weather grows cooler, ladybirds search for a dry, warm place to rest. This can be along windowsills or inside cracks in our homes.

▲ If you find hibernating ladybirds, it is best to move them to a garden shed. In our warm homes they are likely to wake up before spring and then die of hunger.

TOP TIP!

In winter you may see lacewings and some types of butterfly also looking for somewhere dry and warm to spend the winter.

1. Egg

2. Larva

There are far fewer insects around in the winter than in the summer. This is because most insects have their young in the summer months when there is plenty for them to eat.

The usual **lifecycle** of insects is: egg, larva, pupa and adult. Look at page 10 for information about the lifecycle of a housefly.

As the weather cools in the autumn, some types of insect hibernate while most die off, leaving eggs or larvae to survive them through the winter.

4. Adult

3. Pupa

Millipedes

Millipedes sometimes wander into our homes in search of shelter. They are completely harmless and do a good job outside by eating dead plant material and helping it to rot down. Although their name means 'a thousand legs', millipedes usually have several hundred.

▼ There are several different types of millipede but this snake millipede is the type that you are most likely to see inside homes.

The snake millipede can grow up to 3 cm long.

Identification guide

The minibeasts in this identification guide are organised in the order in which they are featured in the book. Other common minibeasts are listed at the end. As there are thousands of different minibeasts, you may need to use a field guide as well.

 Silverfish: This insect has a slim, silvery body covered in scales, and three long 'tails' at the end of its body. It is nocturnal.

Harvestman: A harvestman is an arachnid. It is not an insect and it is not a spider. A spider has two body parts, while a harvestman has one.

 Woodlouse: The woodlouse is a crustacean and has 14 legs and a hard, shiny body.

Bed bug: This insect sucks human blood, while other types of bug suck **sap** out of plants or blood out of other insects.

 Cockroach: The cockroach has a shiny red or brown body with long antennae. There are thousands of different types of cockroach.

Dust mite: A dust mite is a tiny arachnid. It has eight legs and eats dead skin.

Fly: There are thousands of different types of fly. They are all flying insects with one pair of wings. Use a field guide to identify the type.

Wasp: A wasp is a flying insect with two pairs of wings. If wasps feel in danger they will sting, so don't touch!

 Spider: Spiders come in all shapes and sizes but they all have eight legs and a body in two parts. They are arachnids.

 Beetle: There are thousands of different beetles. They are all insects and many can fly. Some eat flower **nectar**, others eat other minibeasts and some eat dead wood.

26

Beetle grub: A grub is the young of a beetle. The woodworm is the name of the grub of the furniture beetle.

Mosquito: The mosquito is a type of fly. The female feeds on animal blood and lays its eggs in water.

Flea: This tiny, wingless insect lives by sucking blood from animals. It usually lives in animal fur.

Ladybird: The ladybird is a flying insect with two pairs of wings. It is a small beetle that eats aphids.

Ant: An ant is a small insect with long antennae. It is related to the wasp and the bee and spends most of its time collecting food to take back to its nest.

Butterfly: The butterfly is a flying insect. It lays eggs that hatch into caterpillars. In time, the caterpillars turn into adult butterflies.

Moth: A moth is a flying insect and is similar to the butterfly. It lays eggs that hatch into larvae, also called caterpillars.

Millipede: The millipede is not an insect but belongs to the same group of animals as the centipede. It eats dead plant material and moves fairly slowly on its many legs.

Daddy-long-legs: This type of fly is also called a crane fly. It has very long legs, hence its name!

Earwig: The earwig is a small, shiny insect that lives usually in dark, damp places such as cracks in wood or walls, or under a stone.

Lacewing: This pale-green insect has long antennae and almost see-through wings. It eats aphids and other small insects.

Headlouse: The headlouse is a tiny insect that lives in human hair. It feeds on human blood and lays eggs in hair.

Glossary

Animals The huge group of living things including birds, insects, mammals, crustaceans, reptiles and amphibians.

Antennae The pair or pairs of bendy threads joined to an insect's head and used for smell, taste and touch.

Aphid An insect that sucks sap out of plants.

Arachnid An animal with eight legs, like a spider, harvestman or mite.

Backbone The line of bones down the middle of the skeleton.

Bacteria The smallest forms of plant life that live everywhere – in soil, water, air and inside our bodies. Some bacteria cause diseases.

Bug The name for an insect with piercing mouthparts, which it uses to suck sap from a plant or blood from an animal.

Crustacean A member of a large group of animals including woodlice. Most other crustaceans live in the sea – crabs, lobsters and shrimps, for example.

Grub The larva of the beetle.

Habitat A place where certain plants and animals like to live.

Hibernate To spend the winter in a state of deep sleep.

Insects A huge group of animals. All insects have a body in three parts – the head at one end, thorax in the middle and abdomen at the other end. Six legs are attached to the thorax and many insects also have wings.

Invertebrates A huge group of animals without a backbone including insects, worms and spiders.

Larva (plural larvae) The stage in the lifecycle of many insects after they hatch from eggs.

28

Lifecycle The lifetime of a living thing, from birth until death. An insect lifecycle often goes through these stages: egg, larva, pupa and adult.

Microscope An instrument that makes very small things appear bigger.

Nectar The sweet liquid made by flowers and eaten by many insects.

Nocturnal Animals that rest during the day and are active at night.

Pest An unwanted insect or other animal.

Pollen A fine powder made by the flower of a plant. It fertilises other flowers.

Pulp A soft, soggy mixture, used to make paper.

Pupa (plural pupae) Part of the lifecycle of many insects before they turn into adults.

Queen In wasps and colonies, the most important insect that lays all the eggs.

Sap The liquid inside a plant.

Websites to visit

www.nhm.ac.uk/kids-only/get-the-facts/facts/cockroaches/crazy-for-cockroaches.html
The Natural History Museum's 'Get the facts' site where you can read about cockroaches and follow links to photos and other information sites.

www.bbc.co.uk/nature/reallywild/features/cc_index.shtml
BBC site about insects.

www.ladybird-survey.org/youth/ladybird_spotters.htm
The children's section of the UK Ladybird Survey has answers to some of the most common questions asked about ladybirds.

Note to parents and teachers:
Every effort has been made by the Publishers to ensure that these websites are suitable for children, that they are of the highest educational value, and that they contain no inappropriate or offensive material. However, because of the nature of the Internet, it is impossible to guarantee that the contents of these sites will not be altered. We strongly advise that Internet access is supervised by a responsible adult.

Index